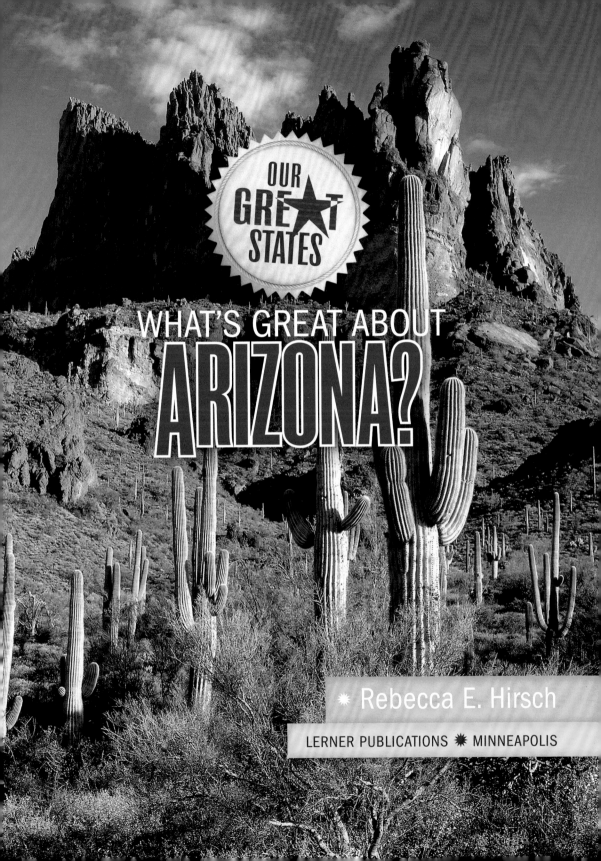

OUR
GRE★T
STATES

WHAT'S GREAT ABOUT
ARIZONA?

✳ Rebecca E. Hirsch

LERNER PUBLICATIONS ✳ MINNEAPOLIS

CONTENTS

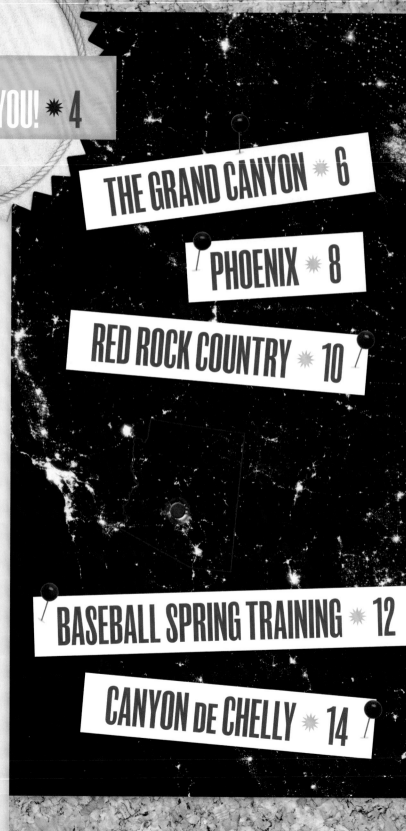

Content Consultant: Thomas J. Davis, PhD, JD, Professor of History, Arizona State University

Lerner Publications Company
A division of Lerner Publishing Group, Inc.
241 First Avenue North
Minneapolis, MN 55401 USA

For reading levels and more information, look up this title at www.lernerbooks.com.

Main body text set in ITC Franklin Gothic Std Book Condensed 12/15.
Typeface provided by Adobe Systems.

Library of Congress Cataloging-in-Publication Data

Hirsch, Rebecca E.
    What's great about Arizona? / by Rebecca E. Hirsch.
        pages   cm. — (Our great states)
    Includes index.
    ISBN 978-1-4677-3862-0 (library binding : alkaline paper)
    ISBN 978-1-4677-6264-9 (eBook)
    1. Arizona—Juvenile literature. I. Title.
F811.3.H57 2015
979.1—dc23   2014018124

Manufactured in the United States of America
1 – PC – 12/31/14

ARIZONA Welcomes You!

Welcome to Arizona, home of the Grand Canyon! People in Arizona love to enjoy the outdoors. Go hiking near the city of Sedona or horseback riding in Monument Valley. Count how many giant saguaro cacti you see. Arizona is home to rich American Indian and Spanish-speaking cultures. Visit American Indian ruins at Canyon de Chelly. Check out one of the many rodeos held in Arizona. There is so much to see and do in this state. Read on to learn ten things that make Arizona great!

ARIZONA

THE GRAND CANYON STATE
WELCOMES YOU

Explore Arizona's parks and all the places in between! Just turn the page to find out about the GRAND CANYON STATE. >

THE GRAND CANYON

> Grand Canyon National Park is a great place to start your trip to Arizona. The canyon is so big that it can be seen from space! In some places, it is as deep as 1 mile (1.6 kilometers) below sea level. It is also 277 miles (446 km) long. Try to be at the canyon at sunrise or sunset. You'll be wowed by all the colors in the rocks.

If you like trains, hop aboard the Grand Canyon Railway. This 130-mile (209 km) ride takes you from the town of Williams to the canyon's South Rim and back. The train has a glass roof and stunning views of the canyon and wildlife. You may see elk, mountain lions, or bald eagles.

At the South Rim, walk the Trail of Time exhibit. This rock timeline shows the canyon's history. See rocks and read trail signs to learn more about how the Grand Canyon formed.

If you're looking for more adventure, ride a mule into the canyon! At the North Rim, choose from mule rides that last from one hour to one day. Guides ride along and tell you about the canyon.

FORMING THE GRAND CANYON

The Grand Canyon was
formed by the Colorado River.
The fast-moving water washed
away loose dirt and rocks.
Over time, the river has sliced
deeper and deeper into the
rock. The Colorado River
has been carving the Grand
Canyon for six million years.

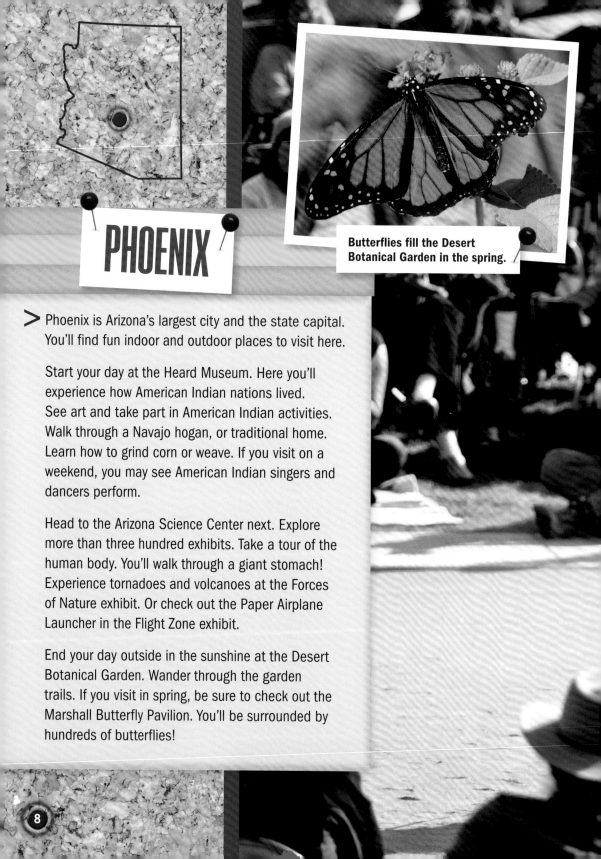

PHOENIX

Butterflies fill the Desert Botanical Garden in the spring.

> Phoenix is Arizona's largest city and the state capital. You'll find fun indoor and outdoor places to visit here.

Start your day at the Heard Museum. Here you'll experience how American Indian nations lived. See art and take part in American Indian activities. Walk through a Navajo hogan, or traditional home. Learn how to grind corn or weave. If you visit on a weekend, you may see American Indian singers and dancers perform.

Head to the Arizona Science Center next. Explore more than three hundred exhibits. Take a tour of the human body. You'll walk through a giant stomach! Experience tornadoes and volcanoes at the Forces of Nature exhibit. Or check out the Paper Airplane Launcher in the Flight Zone exhibit.

End your day outside in the sunshine at the Desert Botanical Garden. Wander through the garden trails. If you visit in spring, be sure to check out the Marshall Butterfly Pavilion. You'll be surrounded by hundreds of butterflies!

Students explore the Forces of Nature exhibit in the Arizona Science Center.

RED ROCK COUNTRY

> You won't want to miss the beautiful city of Sedona on your Arizona trip. The town sits in Red Rock Country. Here, layers of stone form bands of red. This is how the area got its name.

Oak Creek Canyon is one of the best drives to explore. Stop at Oak Creek Vista. Take in the view of the canyon rocks. Shop for crafts from American Indian artists. Have a picnic or explore on foot. Try the West Fork Trail. It winds along a stream and into a narrow red rock canyon. You may be hot after hiking. Grab your bathing suit and head over to Slide Rock State Park. Splash in the creek to cool down.

If you like animals, visit the nearby Out of Africa Wildlife Park. Feed the giraffes and get close to wild animals on an African bush safari. You can also watch tigers do tricks or pet a giant snake.

End your day with stargazing. Arizona is famous for its star-filled skies. Hire a guide to give you a tour of the sky using a powerful telescope.

Take a ride down the 30-foot (9-meter) natural water slide in Slide Rock State Park.

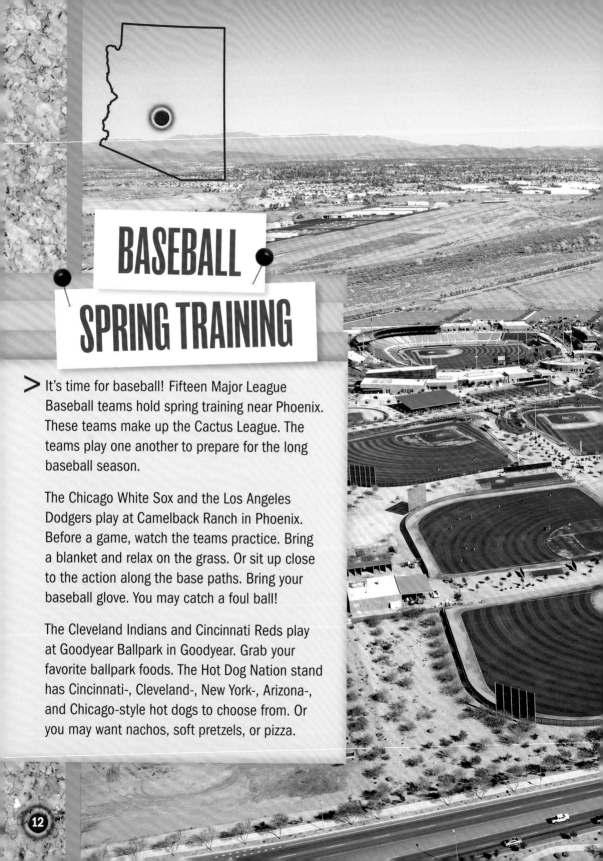

BASEBALL SPRING TRAINING

> It's time for baseball! Fifteen Major League Baseball teams hold spring training near Phoenix. These teams make up the Cactus League. The teams play one another to prepare for the long baseball season.

The Chicago White Sox and the Los Angeles Dodgers play at Camelback Ranch in Phoenix. Before a game, watch the teams practice. Bring a blanket and relax on the grass. Or sit up close to the action along the base paths. Bring your baseball glove. You may catch a foul ball!

The Cleveland Indians and Cincinnati Reds play at Goodyear Ballpark in Goodyear. Grab your favorite ballpark foods. The Hot Dog Nation stand has Cincinnati-, Cleveland-, New York-, Arizona-, and Chicago-style hot dogs to choose from. Or you may want nachos, soft pretzels, or pizza.

After the game, hang around to get autographs from your favorite players *(above)*. The Cincinnati Reds mascots pose before a spring training game *(right)*.

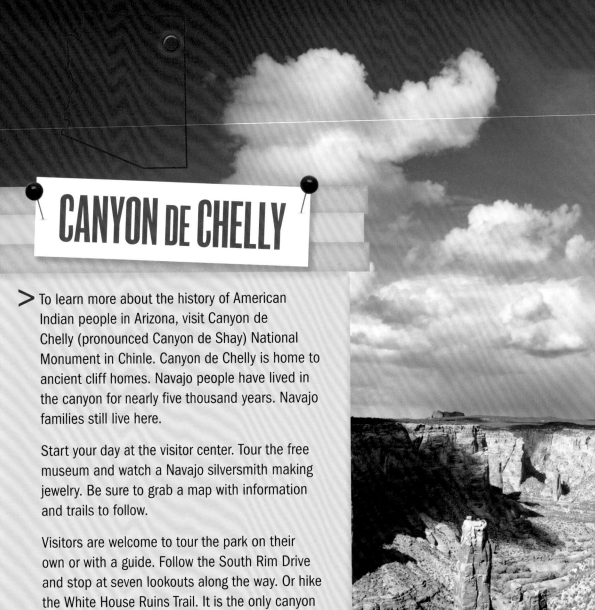

CANYON DE CHELLY

> To learn more about the history of American Indian people in Arizona, visit Canyon de Chelly (pronounced Canyon de Shay) National Monument in Chinle. Canyon de Chelly is home to ancient cliff homes. Navajo people have lived in the canyon for nearly five thousand years. Navajo families still live here.

Start your day at the visitor center. Tour the free museum and watch a Navajo silversmith making jewelry. Be sure to grab a map with information and trails to follow.

Visitors are welcome to tour the park on their own or with a guide. Follow the South Rim Drive and stop at seven lookouts along the way. Or hike the White House Ruins Trail. It is the only canyon floor trail you can hike without a Navajo guide. You'll see American Indian houses along the trail. Continue following the trail to see the White House Ruins up close. This site gets its name from a long white wall within the ruins. If you're looking for a more relaxed tour, take a guided jeep trip around the canyon.

You may see ancient drawings made by the Navajo people.

You will see the White House ruins at the end of the White House Ruins Trail.

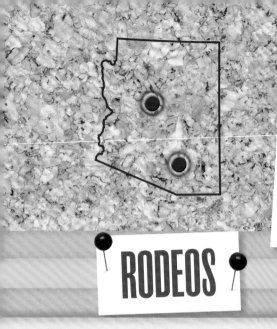

RODEOS

> Dust off your blue jeans and cowboy boots. An Arizona rodeo is a perfect spot to experience Wild West entertainment.

In July, enjoy the World's Oldest Rodeo at Prescott Frontier Days. This rodeo started in 1888. Enjoy the rodeo parade and some barbecue. Ride the ponies or see how long you can hold on to a mechanical bull. The best part of Frontier Days is watching top athletes compete in events such as bull riding and barrel racing. Cowgirls make sharp turns on horseback around barrels in the barrel-racing event.

Other rodeos occur throughout the year. The nine-day La Fiesta de los Vaqueros takes place each February in Tucson. The Tucson Rodeo Parade has horses, bands, and performers. More than 150,000 people line the street to watch each year. Tucson schools even close on parade day! The Tucson Rodeo has more than 650 cowboys from the United States and Canada.

VÁSQUEZ DE CORONADO

In 1540, Spanish explorer Francisco Vásquez de Coronado came to the southwestern United States. He is known for leading the first organized group of Europeans who traveled to this area. Vásquez de Coronado was searching for cities of gold, but he found Pueblo villages instead. Vásquez de Coronado and his explorers continued to look for treasure. They found the Grand Canyon and the Colorado River, but they never found gold.

17

MONUMENT VALLEY

> Monument Valley in Apache County is a must-see stop. The valley has huge sandstone rocks called mesas and buttes.

The valley is part of the Navajo Nation. The Navajo name for it is *Tse'Bii'Ndzisgaii*, or "the valley within the rocks." Monument Valley was once flat, but wind and water slowly wore away the rock. This left behind the sandstone towers.

At the Monument Valley visitor center, sign up to take a tour on horseback. A Navajo guide leads the ride and talks about the valley. Try to visit at sunset, when the rocks glow with the colors of fire.

Just down the road from the visitor center, stop along the roadside. Navajo vendors sell arts, crafts, souvenirs, and food.

Four Corners Monument is 100 miles (161 km) from Monument Valley. This is the only place where four US states meet at one point. Have a hand or a foot in Arizona, Colorado, New Mexico, and Utah at the same time.

Four Corners Monument is also part of the Navajo Nation.

PUEBLO AMERICAN INDIANS

From 100 to 1600 CE, ancient Pueblo lived in the Four Corners area. They built multistory buildings from adobe, a material made from sun-dried clay and straw. They used ladders to climb between floors.

Many of their villages are built into cliffs. The ancient Pueblo are the ancestors of today's Pueblo.

TUCSON

> You'll find plenty to see and do in the city of Tucson. It is in the Sonoran Desert. This desert covers southwestern Arizona.

Start at the Pima Air & Space Museum. You'll see more than three hundred historic aircraft, including a replica of the *Wright Flyer*. This was the first airplane flown by Orville and Wilbur Wright. In 1903, these brothers were the first to successfully fly an airplane. Sign up for a tour of the airplanes at the museum. Don't miss the Boneyard tour. You'll get to see a graveyard of old airplanes.

Head to downtown Tucson for lunch. There you'll find El Charro Café, the country's oldest Mexican restaurant. It has been open since 1922. Try a chimichanga, which is a tortilla wrapped around meat and deep-fried. The restaurant claims to have invented this famous Arizona food!

After stopping for lunch, visit the Arizona-Sonora Desert Museum. You'll see wild mountain lions, prairie dogs, and coyotes. Pet a gopher snake. Get up close to hummingbirds at the Hummingbird Aviary. Then wander through forests of saguaro cacti at Saguaro National Park.

SAGUARO CACTUS

The saguaro cactus is found only in the Sonoran Desert. Many desert animals depend on saguaro cacti. Birds, bats, and insects drink the nectar of its flowers. Tortoises and coyotes eat its bright red fruit. Rats, deer, and bighorn sheep eat the cactus itself. The Gila woodpecker drills a hole in the cactus and builds its nest inside. When a woodpecker moves out, other birds may move in.

A coyote is one of the many wild animals you may see at the Arizona-Sonora Desert Museum.

ROUTE 66

> Take a drive into the United States' past. Route 66 was the country's first paved cross-country highway. It runs all the way from Chicago, Illinois, to Los Angeles, California. More of this famous road passes through Arizona than any other state. Tune your radio to KZKE 103.3 and listen to music from the 1960s, when Route 66 was known as the Main Street of America.

Visit the gold-mining town of Oatman. Shop for souvenirs in this classic Wild West town. Enjoy the burros, or small donkeys, that wander the streets.

When you get hungry, grab a bite at Delgadillo's Snow Cap Drive-In. Enjoy a burger and a root beer float on the patio. Beware! The owners like to play tricks on the customers. The door to the restaurant has two knobs, but only one works!

Watch out for the burros in Oatman. They can bite!

The first owner of Delgadillo's decorated this car to get attention for his restaurant.

HOOVER DAM AND LAKE MEAD

> End your trip to Arizona at one of the most impressive human-made structures on Earth. The Hoover Dam sits on the Colorado River on the Arizona and Nevada state line. The dam has enough concrete to build a 4-foot-wide (1.2 m) sidewalk around the world!

Before the dam was built, the Colorado River flowed freely through Black Canyon. Construction on the dam began in 1931. More than twenty thousand people worked on the dam before it was completed in 1936. Snap some photos from the top of the dam. Take the Powerplant Tour to go deep into the dam and learn how it was built.

The dam created the 110-mile-long (177 km) Lake Mead. This enormous desert lake is the largest reservoir in the United States. You can go boating, fishing, or swimming. Along the shores, you'll find plenty of desert wildlife. You may see roadrunners or bighorn sheep.

Stop in the visitor center for more Information on the history of the dam.

FOOD & GIFTS

Lake Mead holds about 9 trillion gallons (34 trillion liters) of water!

YOUR TOP TEN!

You've read about ten fun things to see and do in Arizona. Now it's your turn! What would your Arizona top ten list include? Grab a sheet of paper and make your own Arizona top ten list. What would be your favorite places to visit? What would you do there? Turn your list into a book. Illustrate it with your own drawings or pictures from the Internet.

NEVADA

UTAH

C O L O R A D O   P L A T E A U

Lake
Mead

**Grand
Canyon**

Colorado River

Grand Canyon
National Park

Little Colorado River

P A I N T E D   D E S E R T

Monument
Valley

Canyon
de Chelly

Hoover
Dam

Humphreys Peak
(12,633 feet/
3,851 m)

World's Oldest
Rodeo
(Prescott)

Sedona

N

Miles
0   20   40

0   20   40   60
Kilometers

CALIFORNIA

Colorado River

M O G O L L O N   R I M

SONORAN
DESERT

Surprise

Peoria

Glendale

Scottsdale

Phoenix

Mesa

Gilbert

Tempe

Chandler

Gila River

⬤ **Arizona Science Center**

⬤ **Heard Museum**

⬤ **Desert Botanical Garden**

Saguaro
National
Park

Tucson

⬤ **Pima Air & Space
Museum**

⬤ **La Fiesta de
los Vaqueros**

⬤ **Arizona-Sonora
Desert Museum**

M E X I C O

USA
MEXICO

ARIZONA BY MAP

> MAP KEY

⭐ Capital city

◯ City

◉ Point of interest

▲ Highest elevation

–··– International border

–·– State border

— Route 66

ᵕᵕᵕᵕ Grand Canyon

Visit www.lernerresource.com to learn more about the state flag of Arizona.

ARIZONA FACTS

NICKNAME: The Grand Canyon State

SONGS: "Arizona March Song" by Margaret Rowe Clifford and "Arizona" by Rex Allen Jr.

MOTTO: *Ditat Deus*, or "God Enriches"

FLOWER: saguaro cactus blossom

TREE: paloverde

BIRD: cactus wren

ANIMALS: Arizona tree frog, ringtail, ridge-nosed rattlesnake

FOOD: chimichanga

DATE AND RANK OF STATEHOOD: February 14, 1912; the 48th state

CAPITAL: Phoenix

AREA: 113,991 square miles (295,235 sq. km)

AVERAGE JANUARY TEMPERATURE: 41°F (5°C)

AVERAGE JULY TEMPERATURE: 80°F (27°C)

POPULATION AND RANK: 6,626,624; 15th (2013)

MAJOR CITIES AND POPULATIONS: Phoenix (1,488,750), Tucson (524,295), Mesa (452,084), Chandler (245,628), Glendale (232,143)

NUMBER OF US CONGRESS MEMBERS: 9 representatives, 2 senators

NUMBER OF ELECTORAL VOTES: 11

NATURAL RESOURCES: copper, molybdenum concentrates, sand, gravel, silver, cement

AGRICULTURAL PRODUCTS: beef cattle, cotton, hay, lettuce, melons, milk

MANUFACTURED GOODS: chemicals, computer and electronics equipment, processed foods, transportation equipment

STATE HOLIDAYS AND CELEBRATIONS: American Family Day, Constitution Commemoration Day

GLOSSARY

adobe: a building material made of sun-dried clay and straw

butte: a flat-topped hill with steep sides that is narrower than a mesa

canyon: a deep, narrow valley with steep sides

desert: dry land with little rainfall

hogan: a Navajo American Indian home usually made of logs and mud

mesa: a flat-topped hill with steep sides

replica: a close copy of the original

reservoir: a lake where water is collected as a water supply

saguaro cactus: a cactus found only in the Sonoran Desert

sandstone: a rock made of sand and held together by a natural cement

silversmith: a person who crafts objects from silver

LERNER

SOURCE

Expand learning beyond the printed book. Download free, complementary educational resources for this book from our website, www.lernerresource.com.

FURTHER INFORMATION

Arizona Secretary of State Kids Page
http://www.azsos.gov/public_services/kids/kids_state_symbols.htm
Learn fun facts about Arizona's state symbols, nickname, and state history.

Arizona-Sonora Desert Museum: Sonoran Desert Digital Library for Kids
http://www.desertmuseumdigitallibrary.org/kids
At this jam-packed site, you can watch videos about the animals of the Sonoran Desert, hear animal sounds, and play games such as desert zoodoku.

Cunningham, Kevin, and Peter Benoit. *The Navajo*. New York: Scholastic, 2011. Learn about Navajo culture and history.

National Geographic: Grand Canyon
http://travel.nationalgeographic.com/travel/national-parks /grand-canyon-quiz
Take this fun quiz and test your knowledge of the Grand Canyon, its wildlife, and how the canyon was formed.

Storad, Conrad J., and Lynda Exley. *Arizona Way Out West & Wacky: Awesome Activities, Humorous History, and Fun Facts!* Chandler, AZ: Five Star Publications, 2012. This fun book is filled with wacky stories and facts about Arizona, along with puzzles, coloring pages, games, recipes, and crafts.

Zuehlke, Jeffrey. *The Grand Canyon*. Minneapolis: Lerner Publications, 2010. Learn more about the Grand Canyon, the people who visit it, and how the canyon was formed.

INDEX

PHOTO ACKNOWLEDGMENTS

The images in this book are used with the permission of: © Bernadette Heath/Shutterstock Images, p. 1; NASA, pp. 2–3; © Laura Westlund/Independent Picture Service, pp. 4, 26–27; © Janece Flippo/Shutterstock Images, p. 5; © Prochasson Frederic/Shutterstock Images, pp. 4–5; © Greg Vaughn/Alamy, p. 6; National Park Service, pp. 6–7, 7; © Jamescking3/Shutterstock Images, p. 8; © Jack Kurtz/Zuma Press/Newscom, pp. 8–9; © Mark Gibson Danita Delimont Photography/Newscom, p. 9; © Caters News/Zuma Press/Newscom, p. 10; © Michael Warwick/Shutterstock Images, pp. 10–11; © Dave G. Houser/Alamy, p. 11; © Tim Roberts Photography/Shutterstock Images, pp. 12–13; © Keith Birmingham/Zuma Press/Icon SMI, p. 13 (left); © Bill Florence/Shutterstock Images, p. 13 (right); © Galyna Andrushko/Shutterstock Images, pp. 14–15; © ala737/Shutterstock Images, p. 15 (left); © Steve Byland/Shutterstock Images, p. 15 (right); © Robert Harding Picture Library Ltd/Alamy, p. 16; © Jack Kurtz/UPI Photo Service/Newscom, pp. 16–17; © Blue Lantern Studio/Corbis, p. 17; Library of Congress, pp. 18 (LC-DIG-highsm-15760), 18–19 (LC-DIG-highsm-04240), 19 (LC-USZ62-46952), 21 (top) (LC-DIG-highsm-04446), 22–23 (LC-DIG-highsm-04936), 23 (left) (LC-DIG-highsm-04939); © Jorg Hackemann/Shutterstock Images, pp. 20–21; © Nelson Sirlin/Shutterstock Images, p. 21 (bottom); © mlkcorp/Shutterstock Images, p. 23 (right); © Andrew Zarivny/Shutterstock Images, pp. 24–25, 29 (bottom right); © Chris Curtis/Shutterstock Images, p. 25 (top); © Domenic Gareri/Shutterstock Images, p. 25 (bottom); © nicoolay/iStockphoto, p. 27; © Jim David/Shutterstock Images, p. 29 (top right); © Riegsecker/Shutterstock Images, p. 29 (top left); © Natalia Bratslavsky/Shutterstock Images, p. 29 (bottom left).

Cover: Courtesy of the Desert Botanical Gardens, (butterfly); © iStockphoto.com/Sara Winter, (cactus); © iStockphoto.com/jose1983, (Grand Canyon); © Matejh photography/Collection/Thinkstock, (Hoover Dam) © Laura Westlund/Independent Picture Service (map); © iStockphoto.com/fpm (seal); © iStockphoto.com/vicm (pushpins); © iStockphoto.com/benz190 (corkboard)